Fin

Beverly Hoffman and Rebecca E. Shook

Illustrated by Andrew Geeson

DOMINIE PRESS
Pearson Learning Group

Here is a cat.

Can you find the cat?

Here is a dog.

Can you find the dog?

Here is a car.

Can you find the car?

Here is a tree.

Can you find the tree?

Here is a bike.

Can you find the bike?

Here is a train.

Can you find the train?

Here is a bird.

Can you find the bird?

ISBN 1-56270-859-7

Printed in Singapore
4 5 6 7 8 9   07 06 05

Dominie
Press
Pearson Learning Group

1-800-321-3106
www.pearsonlearning.com